To the Reader . . .

"World Cities" focuses on cities as a way to learn about the major civilizations of the world. Each civilization has at its roots the life of one or more cities. Learning about life in the great cities is essential to understanding the past and present of the world and its people.

People live in cities for many reasons. For one thing, they value what cities can offer them culturally. Culture thrives in all cities. It is expressed in visual arts, music, and ethnic celebrations. In fact, a city's greatness is often measured by the richness of culture that it offers those who live there.

Many people choose to live in cities for economic reasons. Cities offer a variety of jobs and other economic opportunities. Many city dwellers have found prosperity through trade. Nearly all the world's great cities were founded on trade—the voluntary exchange of goods and services between people. The great cities remain major economic centers.

City living can, of course, have its disadvantages. Despite these disadvantages, cities continue to thrive. By reading about the people, culture, geography, and economy of various metropolitan centers, you will understand why. You will also understand why the world is becoming more and more urban. Finally, you will learn what it is that makes each world city unique.

Mark Schug, Consulting Editor
Co-author of *Teaching Social Studies in the Elementary School* and *Community Study*

CONSULTING EDITOR
Mark C. Schug
Professor of Curriculum and Instruction
University of Wisconsin-Milwaukee

EDITORIAL
Amy Bauman, Project Editor
Barbara J. Behm
Judith Smart, Editor-in-Chief

ART/PRODUCTION
Suzanne Beck, Art Director
Carole Kramer, Designer
Thom Pharmakis, Photo Researcher
Eileen Rickey, Typesetter
Andrew Rupniewski, Production Manager

Reviewed for accuracy by:
Salomon Flores
Associate Professor of Education
University of Wisconsin-Milwaukee

Toni Griego Jones
Assistant Professor, Curriculum and Instruction
University of Wisconsin-Milwaukee

Quoted material on page 7 from *La Capital: The Biography of Mexico City,* by Jonathan Kandell. Copyright © 1988. Reprinted by permission of Random House, Inc.

Material on page 23 and 58 adapted from *Distant Neighbors: Portrait of the Mexicans* by Alan Riding. Copyright © 1984. Reprinted by permission of Random House, Inc.

Library of Congress Number: 89-10503

1 2 3 4 5 6 7 8 9   93 92 91 90 89

Library of Congress Cataloging in Publication Data

Davis, Jim, 1940-
  Mexico City.
  (World cities)

  Summary: Explores the history, cultural heritage, demographics, geography, and economic and natural resources of Mexico City.
  1. Mexico City (Mexico)—Juvenile literature. [1. Mexico City (Mexico)] I. Hawke, Sharryl Davis. II. Title. III. Series: Davis, Jim, 1940- . World cities.
F1386.D38 1989   917.2'53   [B] [92]   89-10503
ISBN 0-8172-3029-7 (lib. bdg.)

Cover Photo: D. Donne Bryant Stock

94931

MEXICO CITY

WORLD CITIES

JAMES E. DAVIS
AND
SHARRYL DAVIS HAWKE

RAINTREE PUBLISHERS
Milwaukee

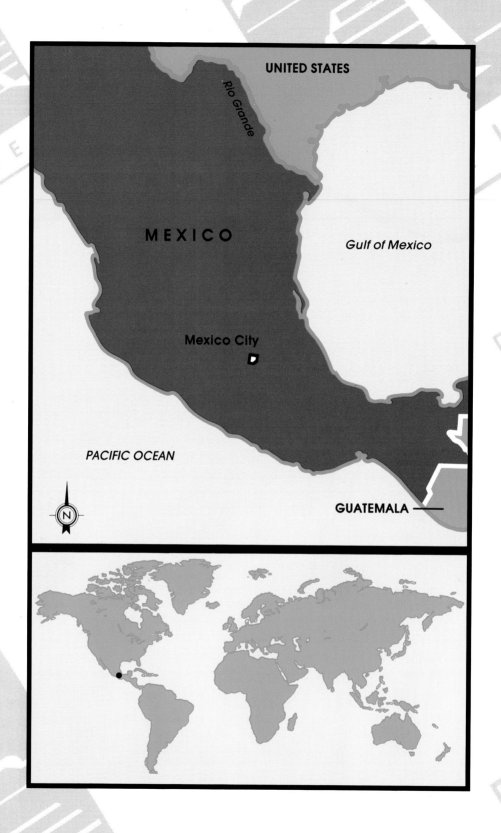

Contents

Introduction

When the Spanish conquistadores first saw the Aztec city of Tenochtitlán (modern-day Mexico City) in 1519, they marveled at its beauty. The white city shimmered against a backdrop of green mountains. A detailed description of the early city is found in the book *La Capital:* "Every building—from modest adobe houses to the stone villas and palaces—was plastered with lime. Trees bordered the cobbled streets and canals. Thousands of Aztecs peered through the flowers and shrubbery of their rooftops at the bearded strangers marching below."

After the Spanish conquest, Mexico City became the most important city in the Western Hemisphere. By the 1550s, it had ten times more people than any other town in New Spain, or Mexico. It was the silver capital of the world and had its own printing press, hospital, and university. Mexico City was the only real city in the entire Spanish colony.

Mexico City lies in the center of the country of Mexico. At a lofty elevation of 7,460 feet (2,274 meters), the city sits in a valley surrounded by mountains. The ranges include the Sierra de Pachuca to the north, the Sierra Nevada with two volcanoes to the east, the Serrania del Ajusco to the south, and the Sierra de las Cruces to the west. This valley is an unlikely setting for a major city. The heart of Mexico City sits on a drained lake bed. The marshy soil of the lake bed has caused the city

Sulfur taken from the Popocatépetl Volcano furnished gunpowder for the Spaniards.

The arrival of the Spaniards brought a bloody end to Aztec culture. Here, Montezuma greets Hernán Cortés.

to sink 20 feet (6 m) since 1900. And the surrounding mountains make it difficult to pump water into and sewage out of the city. This great city is located here because of the Aztec Indians and the power of their religious beliefs.

The Aztecs had been searching for an omen that would tell them where to settle and build a city. One day in 1325, they saw a vision over Lake Texcoco in the Valley of Mexico. They laboriously built their city, called Tenochtitlán, on two islands. The fierce and fearless Aztec warriors conquered the Indians around them and established the vast and wealthy Aztec Empire. Montezuma II was their most famous emperor.

In 1521, the Aztecs were conquered by the Spaniards, led by Hernán Cortés. Spain was quick to convert the Indians to Catholicism. In doing this, Cortés destroyed and buried the sacred temples and sacrificial altars of the Aztecs. The Spaniards intermarried with the Aztecs, and their offspring were called mestizos, or Mexicans.

After almost three hundred years of rule by Spain, the Mexicans revolted in 1810. A long, hard battle followed, but by 1821, Mexico won its independence. A century later, in 1910, the bitter Mexican Revolution began. A major cause of the revolution was peasant demands for land reforms. These and other reforms were won, and a constitution was written in 1917. Since 1920, Mexico has had a relatively stable, though undemocratic, government. Control of the country is tightly held by the central government, located in Mexico City. Like Washington, D.C., Mexico City is a federal district. A federal district is an area that a country uses for its center of government.

During the twentieth century, Mexico changed from a primarily agricultural nation, heavily dependent on the United States for manufactured goods, to a more industrial nation. Most of the country's industry is located in Mexico City. The hope for better jobs and a higher standard of living has attracted many rural people to the city. This rural-to-urban movement, along with a high birthrate and improved health care, makes Mexico City the fastest growing city in the world. Today, its population is estimated at 18 million. By the year 2000, Mexico City is expected to be the largest city in the world, with an estimated population of 30 million.

Visitors to Mexico City will see why it is a favorite tourist spot for many Americans and Europeans. Although the climate is favorable all year, many people will want to avoid the winter months. That's when the thermal inversions trap smog in the valley, creating the world's worst air pollution. In a thermal inversion, cold air is trapped close to the ground beneath a layer of warm air. Pollution held in the cold air can't escape into the atmosphere.

The Mexican people are warm and friendly. They welcome visitors to their city and want you to feel at home. You will enjoy the rich culture of Mexico City—the street entertainers and vendors, the art that decorates many of the buildings and even subway stations. But you'll also see the poverty—children, alone or with their mothers, begging on the streets or selling gum to tourists. They are victims of a city with too many people and high unemployment.

You'll see that Mexico City is more than the bullfights and fiestas of the travel posters. You may wonder, as others do, how this city can survive the tremendous pressures of population growth, pollution, and economic hardship. But, as you read, you'll understand that Mexico City's hope for the future lies in the spirit of its people.

Early Indians

What is known of the history of Mexico goes back to 1500 B.C. That's almost 3,500 years ago. Yet archaeologists know that people first came to this area about 40,000 years ago. The first people were migrants from the steppes of Asia. They crossed the Bering Strait, when a land bridge connected what is now the Soviet Union to Alaska and the rest of North America. Over hundreds of years, these people moved down the length of North America. Eventually they came into what is now Mexico.

These migrants survived by hunting and gathering. When the descendants of these migrants learned how to grow corn, they stopped wandering and settled in Mexico.

Pre-Columbian Groups

Once settled, the various Indian groups developed their own ways of life and religions. These early people are called pre-Columbian because they lived before Columbus landed in North America in 1492. This pre-Columbian time is the first of three periods in Mexico's known history. It lasted for about three thousand years, from 1500 B.C. to A.D. 1521. The second period represents the Spanish conquest, from A.D. 1521 to 1810. The third period is that of Mexican independence, from 1810 to the present.

The early Indians worshipped corn. To them, it symbolized the source of life. One old legend says that human beings first came from the corn. Corn is almost as important to Mexicans today as it was to the first settlers. It is part of their daily diet. Many people still use the stone dish and pestle that the ancient Indians used to make corn meal.

The Olmecs

The various Indian groups built their own villages and cities. In 1200 B.C., the Olmecs created the first major civilization, located on the southern coast of Mexico. Their civilization lasted about seven hundred years, and they built three major cities: La Venta, San Lorenzo, and Tres Zapotes. Archaeologists have found beautiful jewelry, pottery, and sculpture made by the Olmecs. The detail of Olmec works has led archaeologists to believe that the Olmecs were very advanced. For example, they also developed a numbering system and understood the number *zero* even before the Romans did. By about 100 B.C., the Olmecs were no longer a powerful force in the Mesoamerican culture. Though they did not abandon their villages, the Olmecs eventually disappeared.

The Zapotecs

The Zapotec Indians settled the region of Oaxaca around 300 B.C. There they flattened a mountaintop and built the city of Monte Albán. This city, which was built between

Francisco Arcaute

A stone face carved by the Olmecs is now on display in the National Museum of Anthropology.

A.D. 1 and 900, was an important religious center. The Zapotecs later moved on to Zaachila, and the Mixtecs moved into the Valley of Oaxaca. The Mixtecs used Monte Albán as a ceremonial burying ground.

Teotihuacán

The most amazing early city was Teotihuacán, just 30 miles (48 kilometers) northeast of Mexico City. About 1,500 years ago, when most European capitals were small villages, Teotihuacán was probably the largest city in the world. It was certainly the largest city in the New World and may have had a population of more than 150,000 people.

Unlike the other early cities of Mex-

11

Teotihuacán was the site of pre-Columbian America's largest settlement.

ico, Teotihuacán was a "melting pot" of various Indian cultures. In fact, the Teotihuacános may even have ruled over all of Mesoamerica at one point. Similarities between this culture and later peoples suggest this.

Despite its size and power, the Teotihuacán Empire collapsed about A.D. 700. From its ruins, archaeologists believe that the city may have been raided and burned. The site of these ruins, including the great pyramids of the Sun and the Moon and many other smaller temples, has great historical value and is one of the most-visited pre-Columbian sites.

The Toltecs

The Toltec culture is one of those thought to have emerged from the Teotihuacán culture. The Toltecs were an important force in central Mexico from A.D. 900-1200. Settling north of present-day Mexico City, the Toltecs built the city of Tula. There they worshipped Quetzalcóatl, a god also known as the Plumed Serpent. The legend of Quetzalcóatl was begun in Teotihuacán, and the god supposedly founded the city of Tula. Quetzalcóatl became an important god in both the Toltec and the Aztec cultures.

Quetzalcóatl is also the name of an important Toltec ruler. The Toltec priests believed that Quetzalcóatl could take a human form. When the Toltec chief, Mixcoatl, was murdered, the priests named his infant son Quetzalcóatl. Quetzalcóatl later avenged his father's death and became the leader of the Toltecs. As a ruler, Quetzalcóatl offended the priests by banning human sacrifices. Although the priests forced him to leave, many people continued to worship Quetzalcóatl as a god. Belief in this god was important in Mexico's history.

The Maya

The Maya were another important Central American Indian group. They may have settled in the Yucatán Peninsula as early as 1500 B.C. Descendants of the Maya still live in this area. At its peak, the Maya culture had a vast empire of city-states. This peak, or classic period, of Maya history took place between A.D. 250-900. During this time, the Maya made great advances in the arts and sciences. Their civilization grew very large and advanced because of these developments.

In about A.D. 900, many of the major Maya cities were suddenly abandoned. Historians can only guess at the reason. The people may have died from disease. Or they may have been driven out by conquerors. Or there may have been a drought that forced them to move. Some historians think that the common people may have rebelled against their rulers, but no definite answer has been found.

The Aztecs

The region that is now the heart of Mexico City was not settled until 1325. Although it was not a likely place to settle, the Aztecs (also called Mexicas) chose to settle there. They believed their gods had chosen this place for them.

An old legend says that the Aztecs had been wandering in search of an omen—an eagle perched on a cactus, holding a snake in its beak. (This

A stone carving shows Quetzalcóatl, a god the Aztecs believed their priests had banished for his opposition to human sacrifice.

Francisco Arcaute

image became the national emblem of Mexico after its independence.) One day in 1325, they saw the omen in the middle of Lake Texcoco. There they built the city of Tenochtitlán on two islands. It is the center of Mexico City today.

The Aztecs were fierce warriors. They battled and conquered many of the surrounding Indian tribes. Within one hundred years of their settlement at Lake Texcoco, the Aztecs had created the largest empire of the pre-Columbian period. In battle, the Aztec warriors tried not to kill their enemies. The conquered Indians were captured and taken back to Tenochtitlán where they were sacrificed on sacred altars. An Aztec warrior's success depended on the number of captives he could claim.

The Aztec culture was also brilliant. The people worked hard to make their city liveable. To enlarge it, they added sludge from the lake bed to the shoreline. They built roads in the shallow lake to connect Tenochtitlán to the mainland. They built aqueducts to carry spring water to the town. (Part of an aqueduct can still be seen on Chapultepec Avenue in Mexico City.) Children of both the rich and the poor attended school. The Aztecs built pyramids and the magnificent Templo Mayor to honor their gods.

They also had a splendid outdoor marketplace in the city of Tlatelolco. There were other marketplaces in the empire, but this was the largest. Sometimes as many as sixty thousand people went to Tlatelolco's marketplace in a single day. There people could buy all the supplies they needed: food, clothing, and medicines. Barbers gave haircuts, and women had stands where they sold tamales, honey-sweetened treats, or dog stew. The marketplace was important to Aztec life.

At one end of the marketplace, judges held court. If a customer thought a merchant had cheated him or her, the merchant was taken to the court. If the merchant was found guilty, he or she was fined. Usually a messenger would go to get the merchant's relatives, who came with goods to pay the fine. Justice was swift, and many crimes, such as public drunkenness, were punishable by death.

Many of the Aztecs lived in simple, one-room houses built of sun-dried bricks. The only furniture they had were the mats on which they slept. These were rolled up during the day. Wealthier people lived in larger houses built of sturdier materials such as stone or cement. Because the Aztecs loved flowers, many of their houses had flower gardens. Some people even kept turkeys, which they fattened to eat on special days. Turkeys and dogs were the only animals raised for meat.

Aztec men, like other Indians, had almost no hair on their faces, so they did not shave. They pierced one nostril in which they wore a nose ornament. Women tinted their skin light yellow and sometimes used black or red dye on their teeth. Almost all young boys trained to become warriors. They also learned a trade, such as jewelry making. Young girls learned to grind corn and to weave and embroider. Children

Calendar stones like this one were used by the Aztecs to keep track of their complicated fifty-two-year time cycle.

were loved by their families, but punishment for misbehavior was harsh. If they disobeyed, they were usually scratched with thorns.

Religion was very important to the Aztecs. They worshiped many gods. Each month of their eighteen-month year had its holy days. Great cele-

This mural by Diego Rivera shows Montezuma presiding over a kingdom of prosperity and peace.

brations with feasting, singing, and dancing were held. People wore their best clothes which were richly embroidered and colorful. The nobility also wore fine jewelry and feathers. Even captives of the Aztecs joined in the dancing, singing, and feasting. Sometimes a captive was dressed to represent an Aztec god. But eventually the captive was taken by priests to an altar to be sacrificed as thousands of people watched. The Aztecs believed their gods demanded human blood in exchange for making the crops grow and other favors.

In 1502, Montezuma II, the great-grandson of Montezuma I, became emperor of the Aztecs. He was a wealthy ruler who lived in splendor. For example, while most Aztecs lived on a simple diet of corn and beans, Montezuma had cooks who prepared three hundred different foods for him every day. He also had fresh fish daily, which was brought from the sea by relays of runners.

Montezuma's palace was also a tribute to his wealth. According to descriptions written by the Spaniards, the palace had more than three hundred rooms surrounding three courts. On the palace grounds, Montezuma had beautiful gardens and statues. Ten lakes were home to his collection of water birds. It took three hundred men to care for the birds, and many more were needed to care for the zoo that was also on the palace grounds. The large zoo had animals from various parts of the world. The zoo was also unique in that it contained people that Montezuma thought were unusual.

WORLD

CITIES

From the Spanish Conquest to the Twentieth Century

In 1519, Spanish ships landed on the coast of Mexico near the modern-day city of Veracruz. A small band of soldiers, led by Hernán Cortés, marched inland toward Tenochtitlán. Cortés, who had heard of the Aztec Empire and its great wealth, meant to find it. He was so determined that he even burned his ships to prevent his soldiers from retreating.

Messengers took word of Cortés to Tenochtitlán. Montezuma feared that Cortés might be the returning god Quetzalcóatl. According to legend, Quetzalcóatl had promised to one day return to the Aztecs. To please the "god," Montezuma sent gifts of gold, silver, and jewels to Cortés, hoping that Cortés would then leave.

But Cortés did not leave. Instead, he began to conquer the Indians and their lands as he continued his march toward Tenochtitlán. Eventually, Cortés formed alliances with some of the Indian tribes he encountered. Although these Indians were afraid of the strange-looking Spaniards who wore beards, carried guns, and rode horses (none of which the Indians had seen before), they disliked the Aztecs even more. Aztec cruelty and their practice of human sacrifice had earned Montezuma and his people many enemies.

When Cortés reached Tenochtitlán, he was richly entertained by Montezuma in his father's palace. After several weeks, however, Cortés arrested Montezuma and seized control of the

Aztec Empire. At first the Aztecs submitted to Cortés. But when one of Cortés's soldiers ordered troops to open fire on a religious ceremony, the Aztec warriors rebelled. Cortés's soldiers fled to the palace and were surrounded by the Aztecs. During the seige, Montezuma died of a blow to the head. Some people say he was murdered by the Spaniards. Others say he was killed by those among his own people who did not want him to rule again.

Cortés and his soldiers were trapped in the palace. They grew hungry and thirsty. After a week of fighting, the Spaniards tried to escape. About four hundred of them died trying to leave the city. Many of them drowned in the city's canals. This historic night is called *La Noche Triste* (The Sad Night).

After he escaped, Cortés organized the Indian tribes that did not like the Aztecs. But in the meantime, the Aztecs suffered from an outbreak of smallpox, a disease brought to the New World by the Spaniards. Many of the Aztecs died. By August 1521, Cortés had again seized Tenochtitlán. He named Mexico and Central America *New Spain*.

As the Spaniards settled Mexico, many of the Aztecs became slaves. Cortés would not allow the Indians into the center of the city. He destroyed many Aztec buildings and temples. Spanish architects and Indian craftsmen built new structures that combined the look of Spanish and Indian buildings. This building style is called Spanish colonial. Many of these buildings still exist in the heart of Mexico City and in other cities that the Spaniards established.

The Spaniards made sweeping changes in the lives of the Indians.

The Old Basilica of Our Lady of Guadalupe was built in 1709 on the site where the Virgin Mary had appeared to a Mexican Indian.

Above is the interior of the New Basilica. This new church replaced the 1709 construction, which had begun to sink on its foundations.

They wanted them to forget their Aztec ways and act like Spaniards. They taught Indian children Spanish handicrafts and required them to learn Spanish, the official language of Mexico today, in addition to their native language. Spain also sent missionaries to Mexico to convert the Indians to Christianity. The conversion was achieved quickly after the Indian Juan Diego claimed he saw a vision of the Virgin Mary. The lady, who called herself Holy Mary of Guadalupe, asked that a shrine be built on the hill where she appeared. The Basilica of Our Lady of Guadalupe now stands on that spot.

The Spanish rulers had outlawed human sacrifice, but in 1596, they began their own form of human sacrifice—the Spanish Inquisition came to New Spain. Non-Christians were burned at the stake in ceremonies led by the archbishop. The place where the executions occurred is now Alameda Park.

It is interesting to compare the conquest of Indians in Mexico with that of Indians in the United States. For example, many of the American colonists settled in the new land as families. Single men could usually find white women to marry, so few married Indian women. It was different in Mexico. The Spanish sent Cortés and a band of soldiers to the country. They did not bring women with them. When the soldiers settled, they kidnapped Indian women, who bore their children. Thus Mexico became a nation of mixed-blood people—part Spanish, part Indian.

Mexican Independence

The Mexican people did not like being ruled by Spain. In 1810, an old priest named Miguel Hidalgo y Costilla struck a blow for Mexican independence. On September 15, Hidalgo made a speech, now called Grito de Dolores ("cry of Dolores"), in which he called for the overthrow of the government. He and his followers freed political prisoners and locked up the colonial rulers. Hidalgo was eventually captured and executed. But the hunger for independence grew. Another priest, José María Morelos, then led the revolution. In 1813, Morelos organized a congress for the struggling country. This group declared Mexico's independence from Spain. Morelos, too, was captured and executed by a Spanish firing squad.

Finally, in 1821, Spain granted Mexico its independence. Colonel Agustín de Iturbide, a Spanish military officer who had aided Mexico in its fight, was named emperor. But he was an unpopular dictator. Iturbide ruled the new government for only ten months before going into exile. A year later, Iturbide returned, planning to make a comeback. He was captured almost immediately and executed.

In 1833, General Antonio López de Santa Anna became president. Santa Anna, who liked to call himself "Most Supreme Highness," was the famous general who defeated the Texas rebels at the Alamo. At the time, Texas was part of Mexico, but many Texans were settlers from the United States. When Santa Anna tried to exert greater control over Texas, Texans rebelled. In a later battle at San Jacinto, Santa Anna was captured and held until he

United States ships bombarded Veracruz during the Mexican-American War. Conflict had broken out over the admission of newly-independent Texas into the union. Mexico still claimed Texas as a territory.

signed a paper granting Texas its independence.

The Mexican government, refused to accept Texas's independence. Although Texas became part of the United States in 1845, Mexicans still considered it part of Mexico. They went to war for it again in 1846. Santa Anna, who was again president, lost once more. In 1847, General Winfield Scott led United States forces into Mexico City. The troops surrounded Chapultepec Castle, a military school. The school's cadets refused to surrender. After three days, they leapt to their deaths, shouting patriotic slogans. They are honored today as Mexico's "boy heroes." After this bitter battle, the United States troops surrounded the National Palace. Santa Anna finally signed the Treaty of Guadalupe, which officially gave Texas, New Mexico, and Arizona to the United States.

The French

The conspiracy of 1810 marks the beginning of Mexican independence. From then on, Mexico remained an independent state except for an unusual three-year period beginning in 1864. In that year, the French emperor Napoleon III decided to conquer Mexico. A French army occupied Mexico, and Napoleon made Maximilian, who was the archduke of Austria, the ruler of Mexico. Maximilian's brief rule is best remembered for its glamour. His wife, Charlotte, turned Chapultepec Castle into a fashionable party spot. Eventually, France withdrew support from Maximilian's government. Maximilian was then captured and executed by a Mexican firing squad in 1867.

The Revolution

In 1876, Porfirio Díaz took control of Mexico. He ruled for more than thirty years. Although he was often considered to be a villain, he led Mexico to economic growth. He was deposed in a revolution that lasted from 1911 to 1917. The revolution was led by Francisco Indalecio Madero, who was aided by Francisco "Pancho" Villa and Emiliano Zapata. The Indian peasants' demand for land reform triggered the revolution. When the Spaniards settled Mexico, they took the best farmland away from the native people. Generations of peasants worked for little pay for rich landowners. After the revolution, the Mexican government turned the land over to the Indians.

When the revolution took place, filmmaking was a new art. Someone in Hollywood got the idea that filming a real battle would work better than hiring actors to pretend. So the filmmakers convinced the Mexican troops to allow a film crew to record several

The harsh rule of Porfirio Díaz provoked the Mexican people to overthrow him.

days' fighting. The soldiers even agreed to stop fighting at sundown because in those days filmmakers didn't have portable lights, so they couldn't film at night. All went as planned, but the film footage of the battle never got into the movie. The film editors decided the battles didn't look real enough.

In 1912, Madero came to power, and Díaz went into exile in Paris. Madero, however, did not make a good president. He was not strong enough to control the many forces that came out of the revolution. In 1913, one of Madero's generals, Victoriano Huerta, overthrew the government. Huerta had Madero arrested and later killed. Huerta then assumed control.

The United States under President Woodrow Wilson did not back Huerta. The country sided with Madero's supporters, who were organized under Venustiano Carranza. In 1914, United States troops seized Veracruz to ensure the delivery of arms to Carranza's men. Mexicans call this battle the Veracruz Massacre. Shortly after, Carranza seized Mexico City. Huerta then fled into exile, taking much of the country's wealth with him.

Despite continued struggle among the revolutionary forces, many people accepted Carranza as Mexico's leader. Under his direction, a constitution was written for Mexico in 1917. The constitution of 1917 brought many of the reforms that the revolutionaries sought. It included a bill of rights that gave Mexican workers the right to strike, a minimum wage, and an eight-hour workday.

The Twentieth Century

The twentieth century has seen many reforms in Mexico. Although 95 percent of the Mexican population is Catholic, the state limited the power of the Church in 1924. Priests were no longer allowed to teach in elementary schools or to speak against the Constitution. The government improved the health care system and greatly reduced the death rate of infants and children with its vaccination program. The government also built schools, even in small villages, and required children to attend school for at least six years.

Industrial economic growth and reforms followed. Mexico had been a heavy consumer of imports from the United States and other industrial nations. It now wanted to become a modern country that could manufacture most of the goods its people needed. Many new manufacturing companies were built in Mexico City. With industrialization came the growth of the middle class—people who made enough money to buy modest houses and cars. Hoping to improve their standard of living, many people moved to the city to work.

The most dramatic economic reform was the Mexican government's takeover of foreign oil companies in the 1930s. These oil companies, which were mostly American and British, had established themselves in Mexico. By the 1930s, the companies were making a great deal of money—most of which was leaving the country. Many Mexican people were resentful of this arrangement and pressured the

Pemex was formed with assets confiscated from foreign oil companies based in Mexico.

government to make changes. In a bold move, the government seized the oil company properties.

In place of the foreign companies, the Mexican government established its own oil corporation, called Pemex. Over the years, the corporation grew strong. In the 1970s, Pemex was especially prosperous. Vast oil reserves were discovered at a marshy site called Reforma near the southeastern city of Villhermosa. But this prosperity didn't last. The value of oil dropped sharply, and Mexico's swelling population strained the economy.

Mexico City Today

In Mexico City today there are not enough jobs for all the people. Many of them flee Mexico and enter the United States as illegal aliens to find work. Most of the people are poor. Half of the houses are built by their occupants and lack toilets and running water. Schools and other public buildings are not heated because winters are generally mild. But, on some days, the temperature dips to freezing. Then children wear coats, hats, and gloves in class.

Many people who come from the countryside to find jobs in the city live in shacks. Someone offers to sell them land in the city, and they eagerly pay the money. But often the seller does not really own the land. It may be public land or belong to someone else. Usually, however, these squatters, as they are called, are allowed to stay. Squatters who have no money sometimes move into caves left by abandoned sand quarries. Some even build shacks in the city dump.

One squatter group calls its community *Esperanza,* which is the Spanish word for "hope." The people live in shacks, but they are glad to be out of the caves. Outside of each shack, flowers grow in tin cans. The squatters hope to some day have plumbing.

Mexico City has over one thousand neighborhoods. One of these neigh-

borhoods, Tepito, is famous for its sports center. Tepito's gymnasium has produced Mexico's best boxers.

The people of another neighborhood, Romita, originally lived in the countryside. They hold on to some of their country ways. For example, they raise flowers, vegetables, rabbits, and chickens on their rooftops.

In other parts of the city, the neighborhoods preserve even older ways. Visitors to the market in Milpa Alta would hear people speaking Mexicano, the old Aztec language. And, in Xochimilco, "floating gardens," or chimampas, can be seen. Chimampas are also part of the Aztec heritage. In a big garden, there are wide spaces between

the rows for the gardener to walk along so he or she can tend the garden. In a chimampa, these spaces are canals, and the gardener uses a raft.

Coyoacán and San Angel are two communities in Mexico City that were once Spanish villages. Both have splendid Spanish colonial buildings and cobblestone streets. San Angel has added modern housing developments, but Coyoacán looks much like it did in the sixteenth century. Coyoacán is a favorite place for writers and artists.

Except in the poorest families, most Mexican women do not work outside the home. Women who want to get jobs are discouraged by their husbands. Some Mexican men feel it

Coyoacán's cobbled streets are crowded with shoppers and pushcart vendors.

would be an insult for their wives to work because people would think they couldn't support their families.

You may be surprised to learn that the Mexican society is fragmented. Skin color divides the Mexican people. The upper classes, criollas, are usually light-skinned people of almost pure Spanish descent. The majority of people are darker-skinned mestizos of mixed Spanish and Indian blood. The full-blooded Indians are the lowest class. Most of them come to Mexico City from rural areas. Many live in poverty because they have little education or training.

25

Children of Mexico City

Being a child in Mexico City is very different from being a child in the United States. The schedule of meals, for example, differs from that in the United States. After breakfast and a mid-morning snack, lunch is usually not eaten until anywhere from 2:00 to 4:00 P.M. Dinner is often not eaten until 8:00 or 9:00 P.M. Meals are usually made from scratch rather than being canned or frozen. Like most children, Mexican children love to snack on candies, soda pop, popsicles, and ice cream. The popsicles contain real fruit, such as watermelon, strawberries, or pineapple. A favorite candy is made from fruit flavored with chili pepper. A special treat is a trip to a local restaurant.

Mexican law requires children to go to school for six years. Even so, poor children must sometimes work to help support their families. They beg on streets or sell gum given to them by the government. Young boys may stand at busy intersections and wash the windshields of cars that stop for a light. Drivers usually give them a few pesos. Some boys go from house to house, asking for work. They wash cars, sweep sidewalks, and so on. Girls from poor families sometimes go to live with wealthy families and do

Uniforms like these are standard dress for Mexican schoolchildren.

Barbara Cerva, DDB Stock

26

The Monument to the Boy Heroes honors cadets who died defending Chapultepec Castle from United States troops.

housework or babysitting.

Some children attend school for half of the day and work the rest of the day. Most parents want their children to get an education because they know it is the only way their children can escape poverty. But one problem is that schools require uniforms, and some parents can't afford them. Each school has its own uniforms: an everyday uniform, a uniform for physical education, and a dress uniform for parades. School children spend many hours practicing to march in parades.

Parents who can afford the cost send their children to private schools where they learn English. Some wealthy Mexicans and high-ranking government officials send their children to the American school in Mexico City. The children are usually driven to school by a chauffeur, and some even have bodyguards who stand watch outside the school to protect the children from being kidnapped.

Both rich and poor Mexicans like to spend their Sunday afternoons on family outings. The favorite escape is Chapultepec Park. There a child can really experience the city's rich history—the place where the "boy heroes" died, the castle from which Maximilian ruled, the tree under which Montezuma rested. With a little imagination, the cars scurrying along Reforma Boulevard become Aztecs paddling their rafts down this former canal.

WORLD

CITIES

The City Today: How It Works and Plays

How would you describe yourself right now? You could say how old you are, whether you're a boy or girl, how tall you are, the color of your eyes, what you like to do, who your friends are, and so on. Now, if you were to describe yourself as you'll be in the year 2000, what would you say? Some things would still be the same, such as the color of your eyes. And there are some things you know will be different. For one thing, you'll probably be taller. But for the most part, it would be hard to predict what you'll be like and what you'll be doing. Your ideas of what you want to do for a living, where you want to live, or whether or not you want to be married, for example, will probably change many times

between now and the year 2000.

The reason it's so hard to make good guesses about your future is that at your age, you're going through rapid changes from childhood to adulthood. In a way, Mexico City is doing the same. The city is changing very fast. So, like you, Mexico City faces an uncertain future. One way to describe the city and how it works is to talk about the things that will probably remain the same and those that are changing.

How the City Works

One feature of Mexican culture that has endured from the beginning is the importance of family life. People in Mexico usually live in extended families—that is, children, parents, grandparents, aunts, uncles, and cousins live under the same roof. The average household size is eight people.

Family strength and pride help keep Mexico City going during troubled times. For example, in a period of high unemployment, the family pulls together to feed and house members who are out of work.

But families also contribute to Mexico City's population pressures. First, Mexico's birthrate is high. Mexican families often have many children. This and a greatly reduced death rate have caused a large increase in population in recent years. Second, families in Mexico City encourage their relatives in rural areas and villages to move to the city. Even though jobs are scarce in the city, the grinding poverty of the countryside is worse. People come to the city in the hope of a better life. They know their families will help them out. About 400,000 people migrate from the countryside to Mexico City each year. That's like adding a city the size of Omaha, Nebraska, to Mexico City every year!

Because of the high birthrate and migration pattern, Mexico City will soon become the largest city in the world. Experts predict that thirty million people will live there by the year 2000. Rapid population growth means that most of Mexico City's environmental, economic, and social problems will continue. These problems include air pollution, water supply problems, inefficient removal of sewage and garbage, unemployment, crime, and lack of medical care.

Most of the air pollution in Mexico City is caused by automobile exhaust. Pollution becomes trapped in the valley and is especially bad during the winter months. Mountains that surround the city prevent winds from blowing the dirty air into the atmosphere. The polluted air is held near the ground by a thermal inversion. In a thermal inversion, cold air is trapped close to the ground beneath a layer of warm air. On some days, pollution is so severe that it poses a health hazard to anyone who goes outside. After the sun has been out for a few hours, the ground and the cold air layer near it

A haze of smog hangs over lines of commuter traffic.

David Ryan, DDB Stock

Much of Mexico's pollution goes unregulated. Here, smoke flows freely from a garbage-burning plant.

are warmed. As the air begins to rise, the pollution does, too.

Mexico City is unable to provide clean drinking water for all its residents. The city's water comes from far away and must be pumped over mountains and down into the valley. In some neighborhoods, people buy water from vendors who travel the streets the way ice cream trucks do in this country. The poor areas have no running water. People may walk for a mile or two to buy pure water.

Sewage and garbage disposal presents a similar problem. Sewage must be piped out of the valley and down the mountains. In areas where there is

no disposal, sewage breeds germs that can cause illness and even death. Garbage pickup is mostly limited to middle-class and wealthy neighborhoods because garbage collectors can sell items that these people throw away. Collectors don't like to pick up garbage in the city's poor sections because people there don't throw away anything of value. Poor people often burn their garbage so it won't attract rats. Burning garbage is another source of air pollution.

The unemployment rate is one indication of the economic health of a city. In 1987, about one-fourth of the working population of Mexico was unemployed. Although building more factories in Mexico City would help the unemployment problem, it would also add to the pollution problem. Mexico City is faced with a big challenge: solve one problem without adding to another.

Inflation, another indicator of economic health, means rising prices. While an economy can usually adjust to gradual inflation, rapid inflation can be damaging. In Mexico, rapid inflation came with the oil boom of the 1970s. Oil and related products are the main exports of Mexico. When world oil prices were high, Mexico's economy boomed. Profits from the sale of oil enabled other industries to develop. New businesses created new jobs in Mexico City. More Mexicans than ever before were able to buy houses and cars. But this rapid growth of the economy ignited inflation. Prices went higher and higher.

The slump in oil revenues suffered during the 1980s has left many people unemployed and with time on their hands.

Francisco Arcaute

By the early 1980s, because of the high oil prices, people around the world sought ways to use less fuel. For example, they bought fuel-efficient cars and insulated their homes. As a result, the demand for oil decreased. Oil prices suddenly dropped. Now another kind of economic crisis resulted in Mexico. Many people lost their jobs; others had their wages reduced. Poverty increased.

Unemployment and inflation also brought an increase in crime. Some people in middle-class and wealthy areas now hire security guards to protect their houses. Not even the streets are safe. For example, a boy walking to school was knocked down by a group of boys who took the new athletic shoes he was wearing. The government of Mexico City is not ignoring these problems. The city's problems just seem to grow faster than they can be brought under control. A former mayor of Mexico City said, "Managing this city is like trying to repair an

Laundry airs over a balcony in a poor neighborhood. Ironwork, such as that seen here, is common in older areas of the city.

Francisco Arcaute

airplane in flight."

An example of the difficulties faced by the city government is its transportation system. The city offers public transportation that is cheap but inefficient. Most people share taxis or use buses. But the city has only half the number of buses it needs. Thus, working people spend several hours a day standing in line waiting for rides. Traffic moves slowly, usually about ten miles per hour, during the day. During the rainy season, traffic can get snarled for hours when traffic signals fail and underpasses flood. Many people also use the subways, which are always crowded. The subway system, completed in 1969, is rather unusual. Its stations are beautifully decorated with Mexican, Spanish, and Indian designs. Also, men ride in cars separate from women and children.

Above: Taxis line up for fares in the Zócalo.
Below: The underground railway is one means of transportation in the city.

David Ryan, DDB Stock

33

A mural by David Alfaro Siqueiros decorates the Cultural Polyforum on Insurgentes Avenue.

How the City Plays

Many roads lead out of Mexico City like bicycle spokes connecting the city to ports and other cities in Mexico. Some of these roads are super highways. Still, most tourists prefer to enter Mexico by air because driving in this country can be risky. In Mexico, a traffic accident is a criminal offense. A driver could spend several months in jail just waiting for trial.

Oil and oil products are Mexico's greatest source of income. Tourism is second. Many of Mexico's visitors come from the United States. The cost of food, entertainment, and lodging is cheap compared with similar costs in the United States. Tourists also help the Mexican economy by buying handcrafted items such as silver and leather goods, glassware, handwoven blankets, and so on.

In some ways, Mexican culture is like American culture. Mexico City has fine theater, music, and museums. In some places, tourists can enjoy American-style nightclubs and discos. But for those who want to experience Mexican culture, it's everywhere. Mariachi musicians, acrobats, and dancers entertain every day on the streets, and the city's buildings are decorated with art and murals. The streets are also packed with vendors who sell everything from sunglasses to pre-Columbian art. (The art pieces, of course, are reproductions. It would be illegal to sell genuine pieces.)

A vegetable seller displays his produce at Amecameca's Sunday market.

Shopping in Mexico City includes modern shopping centers with the sound of ringing cash registers, as well as open-air markets with the sound of merchants calling to shoppers to buy their goods. Mexican merchants like to "haggle." Because they expect the buyer to offer less than the marked price of an item, they mark it higher than the price they really want. The shopper and merchant almost play a game as they try to agree on a price. If the shopper leaves without buying, the merchant may follow him or her down the street, offering a lower price.

Street vendors offer all kinds of treats. The Mexican people especially like ears of corn on sticks. They smear the corn with cream or mayonnaise and sprinkle it with chili pepper. They also like cups of fruit, which they sprinkle with lime juice and chili pepper. Fried chips (including potato chips) are also sold in cups and sprinkled with chili pepper juice. You can see that Mexicans love chili peppers.

Like their American neighbors, Mexicans enjoy picnics and family celebrations. They also love festivals and holidays. Many of the fiestas, as they are called, are religious holidays. But some, such as Cinco de Mayo, are not. *Cinco de Mayo*, which means "May 5" in Spanish, is celebrated on that day each year. On this day in 1862, a Mexican army defeated invading French

Death appears in numerous ironic guises during the November Day of the Dead celebrations.

forces at Puebla, Mexico. Cinco de Mayo honors that victory.

Another non-religious Mexican holiday is Mexican Independence Day, which is held on September 16. On this day in 1810, the Mexicans, led by Miguel Hidalgo, began the fight for freedom. Just as Americans celebrate their independence from England, Mexicans celebrate their independence from Spain.

A most unusual Mexican holiday is the Day of the Dead. This two-day celebration, which is held in Novem-

ber, is an ancient Indian celebration. The ancient Indian people believed that at this time the souls of the dead returned. Many Mexicans still celebrate on this day; it is a happy time. During these two days, cemeteries are as lively as Chapultepec Park on a Sunday afternoon. Streets leading to the cemeteries are lined with vendors selling tacos, fruit, candy skulls, toy skeletons, and marigolds (the Aztec flower of death). Families prepare feasts that include their dead loved ones' favorite foods. Then everyone goes to the cemetery for a picnic. They talk to the spirits and leave food on the graves. Some families even keep watch through the night. It is not a spooky time because Mexicans believe the spirits are friendly and would welcome a good family get-together.

On December 12, Mexicans observe Guadalupe Day. This day celebrates the feast of Our Lady of Guadalupe, the patron saint of Mexico. Thousands of people make pilgrimages to her shrine. The church is packed with pilgrims and Indian dancers and musicians. Many pilgrims follow the custom of crawling on their hands and knees to the statue of Guadalupe.

Christmas is a lively and important holiday in Mexico City, where lights and decorations are everywhere. On the nine nights before Christmas, families act out the posada, or story of

Mary and Joseph's search for a room in Bethlehem. Parties are held after the last posada on Christmas Eve. A favorite activity is breaking the piñata, and children scramble for the gifts and candies that fall out. The exchange of gifts comes later, on January 6, with the celebration of Epiphany. The night before, children set out their shoes to be filled with gifts.

Holy Week and Easter are celebrated with Passion Plays that portray Jesus Christ's crucifixion and resurrection. The day before Easter, people buy papier-mâché figures of Judas,

Market stalls offer colorful piñatas, some in the likenesses of popular cartoon characters.

Jay W. Sharp, DDB Stock

Francisco Arcaute

the man who betrayed Christ. They burn these figures with great rejoicing. Sometimes the Judas figures are filled with fireworks, which add to the excitement.

Mexican holidays and events are filled with music, dancing, puppet shows, traditional foods, and parades.

A matador shows his skills to a crowd at the fifty thousand-seat Plaza Mexico bullring, the world's largest.

Even bullfighting, which was introduced by the Spaniards, starts with a parade. Everyone who takes part in the bullfight, except the bull, is in the parade: picadors on horseback, banderilleros, and, of course, matadors. After the parade, the bull is released into the ring. The job of the picadors and banderilleros is to make the bull angry and ready for a good fight. Their job is as dangerous as the matador's because they must get close enough to the bull to stick it with darts and lances.

Once the bull is angry, the matador enters the ring. He wears tight black pants, a richly embroidered jacket, and a black hat. He carries a sword and a muleta, which is a red cape draped over a stick. The matador waves the muleta at the bull. As the bull charges, the matador steps aside to keep from getting trampled or gored by a horn. He must never run from the bull. If he acts bravely, the crowd shouts "Olé!" If he performs poorly, the crowd boos and throws seat cushions into the ring. The matador puts on quite a show before killing the bull with his sword. When the dead bull is dragged off, another bullfight begins.

Jai alai is another popular sport borrowed from Spain. In this game, players try to catch a hard ball hurled by their opponents. Players use a scoop-shaped racquet, called a cesta, to throw and catch the ball, or pelota. The racquet is strapped to the player's arm. With it, a player can hurl the ball as fast as 150 miles (240 km) per hour. Jai alai can be a very dangerous sport because the ball goes so fast.

Mexicans enjoy many of the same sports Americans do. They like soccer, swimming, boxing, baseball, and football. Mexico City even has an indoor skating rink where figure skating and hockey are becoming popular. And, as mentioned earlier, Mexico City produces some of the country's best boxers.

In 1968, Mexico City hosted the Summer Olympic Games. The government provided excellent facilities for the world's athletes and members of the news media. The games went very smoothly, demonstrating to the world that Mexico City and the government of Mexico could organize a successful, international event.

Mexicans also enjoy television. The studios of Televisa, the country's national television network, are located in Mexico City. Mexicans often watch television programs that come from the United States and other countries. Educational television is also important to the people. It is used to enrich the education of children living in remote villages. It is especially helpful

A mural at El Toreo, the smaller of Mexico City's two bullrings, shows a heroic assembly of matadors.

33 JARDINERO

A street corner newsstand displays a wide array of Spanish-language newspapers and magazines.

in teaching Spanish to the many children whose families continue to speak one of the fifty Indian dialects.

Reading is another important pastime for Mexicans. Because of this, publications of various types are popular. Mexico City has seventeen daily newspapers that reflect numerous political opinions. Like Americans, Mexicans cherish their freedom of expression. Debates over national and international issues are lively and open. Book publishing is also big business in Mexico City. In 1539, the city established the first printing press in the New World. Many books published in Mexico are exported to South America.

Mexico City is a lively place, often exciting and rich with tradition. Despite its widespread poverty and "growing pains," the city represents hope to millions of people. Observers from other countries are usually amazed at the spirit of the people and their ability to overcome great hardship. But how, they wonder, will this great city cope with thirty million people?

WORLD CITIES

Places in the City

Do you know how old your city is? How far would you have to travel to see something built in the fourteenth century? If you lived in Mexico City, you wouldn't have to go far.

Ancient ruins and modern buildings stand side by side in Mexico City. Visitors to Mexico City can see the splendors of seven centuries in a three-mile walk from Zócalo Square to Chapultepec Park. The Zócalo is the heart of the city.

One interesting structure is the National Cathedral, an architectural wonder built in the sixteenth century. It took one hundred years to build. Inside the cathedral is a legendary black statue of Jesus Christ. The story is told that someone once tried to murder a bishop by putting poison on the statue. When the bishop knelt to kiss the statue's feet, the statue shriveled and turned black, and the bishop's life was saved. The cathedral stands (or leans) next to the Sagrario, a parish church built several centuries after the cathedral was built. The heavy buildings have sunk into the soft lake bed under the city so that they now lean against one another.

Behind the cathedral are the ruins of the Templo Mayor, built by the Aztecs. The temple was once the center of the Aztec Empire. The temple square once held seventy-eight temples, schools, and palaces. The site had been lost for several centuries until it was unearthed in 1978.

Southwest of the Zócalo is the National Palace where the president of Mexico and other officials have their offices. It stands on a place where the Aztec palace once stood and Montezuma once lived. Part of the National Palace is a museum. The museum holds many ancient art treasures, but its most outstanding feature is a huge mural by the Mexican artist Diego Rivera. The mural illustrates Mexico's history. It covers an entire wall and is several stories high. The Mexican Independence Bell is also located in the National Palace. Every year on the night of September 15, the president of Mexico rings the bell to announce the eve of Independence Day.

Another grand-looking building near the Zócalo actually houses the National Pawnshop. A pawnshop is a type of shop that loans people money in exchange for personal items. If the borrower does not repay the money in a certain period of time, the pawnshop sells the merchandise. At the National Pawnshop, people can buy watches, furniture, cameras, and even gravestones. The site of the National Pawnshop once held the Aztec palace where Cortés and his army were guests of Montezuma in 1519. It is also the place where Montezuma was killed.

The architecture of the area blends old and new. Near the subway station

The National Palace (left) is the seat of Mexican government. Inside is a mural by Diego Rivera showing scenes from Mexican history (below).

Photos from DDB Stock

A pottery shop displays an assortment of colorful lacquer ware.

at the corner of Piño Suarez and Corregidora, an Aztec pyramid can be seen. This pyramid was discovered when the subway was built. Modern hotels stand beside old buildings from Spanish colonial days. Some of the older buildings were modernized to become hotels before the 1968 Summer Olympics.

Not far from the Zócalo is the Casa de los Azulejos, or "House of Tiles," built in the sixteenth century. The outside of the building is covered with blue and white tile. Inside is Sanborn's, a popular, high-quality variety store. Sanborn's offers souvenirs, jewelry, clothing, and even ice cream from the soda fountain.

Across the street is the modern Latin American Tower. It is forty-two stories high and until recently was the tallest building in Mexico City. Mexicans used to boast it was the highest skyscraper in the world because it starts at 7,300 feet (2,225 m). (All of Mexico City lies at this altitude.) From the top of the tower, you can see two snowcapped mountains to the southeast. They have long Indian names: Popocatépetl and Ixtaccihuatl. But people usually call them by their nicknames of *Popo* and *Ixty*. These mountains are actually volcanoes, but they have not erupted for a long time. Both stand over 17,000 feet (5,182 m) tall.

Not far from the Latin American

Visitors can enjoy nightlife in the Zona Rosa, or . . .

. . . go rowing in Chapultepec Park.

Tower on Avenida Juarez is Alameda Park. It is often compared to New York's Central Park. When it was first built in the early seventeenth century, it was open only to wealthy people. After Mexico declared its independence in 1821, the park was opened to the public. The park features great statues and monuments and is a favorite place for family picnics. Concerts are held in its bandstands, and in the nearby Palace of Fine Arts (Palacio de Bellas Artes) the Ballet Folklorico performs on Sunday mornings.

Numerous craft shops line the street across from Alameda Park. Avenida Juarez ends in a *gloriets,* the Mexican name for a traffic circle. Here is where the old city ends and the new one begins. Continuing along Paseo de la Reforma, you'll find the Zona Rosa. This area—a large boulevard with ele-

gant shops and hotels catering to tourists from around the world—stretches to Chapultepec Park.

The site of the Chapultepec Park was once the home of the Emperor Maximilian. Maximilian hired the architect of the famous Champs Élysées in Paris to build the Paseo de la Reforma. Walking along this street, it is easy to imagine the emperor passing by in his carriage as he goes to his offices in the National Palace in the Zócalo. Even longer ago, the Aztecs traveled the same route by raft and canoe, because at one time this huge avenue was a canal.

Vast Chapultepec Park provides a relaxing escape from the city's bustle. Giant cypress trees offer relief from the hot sun. These trees are more than 599 years old. One tree, which stands over 200 feet (61 m) tall, is called

Montezuma. The Aztec ruler liked to sit under this tree when it was just a sapling. Street vendors in the park offer a tempting display of fresh fruit, usually served with lime juice. Chapultepec Park is a favorite place for celebrating events such as birthdays. You may see an area roped off with balloons in which children are lined up to break the piñata, a traditional birthday game.

Besides its fresh air, trees, and street vendors, Chapultepec Park has some outstanding museums. The most remarkable is the National Museum of Anthropology. Each of its ten halls features a different civilization. In the museum, you can see how people live today in Mexico and how they lived in the past. The museum has an ancient Aztec calendar. It is carved into a stone that weighs twenty tons and is 12 feet (4 m) wide.

The park also has a zoo, a roller rink, a botanical garden, a lake, and

A statue outside the National Museum of Anthropology reflects Mexico's pride in its Aztec past.

Francisco Arcaute

Chapultepec Castle was once the home of the vice-regent, the highest official of Spain in the New World.

several old buildings. One of these buildings is Chapultepec Castle, built in the eighteenth century. It was a military school in 1847 when American General Winfield Scott attacked and captured Mexico City. The school's cadets leapt from the building to their deaths rather than surrender. The Monument to the Boy Heroes, which stands in the park, honors the cadets who died so bravely in the invasion.

After a day of exploring the old and new wonders of Mexico City, you'll probably be too tired to walk anywhere else. Walking at 7,300 feet (2,225 m) above sea level is tiring. The air at this altitude is very thin. It has less oxygen than air at lower altitudes so your heart must work harder to get oxygen to your cells. But it's worth the effort when you stop to think you've explored seven centuries of history in one day.

WORLD
CITIES

The City's Surroundings

Although a trip to Mexico City is extraordinary in itself, the wonders are multiplied when you take time for bus or car excursions outside the city. The area around Mexico City is not only rich with history and culture; it is also interesting for its natural features.

Natural Features

Set on a high plateau, the city is surrounded by mountains. Two of the tallest peaks are actually the volcanoes Popocatépetl and Ixtaccihuatl. Flowers and cacti grow practically everywhere. They thrive in the mild climate. Days are warm year round, even in the rainy season from May to October. During these months, it rains almost every day, but only in late afternoon. The winter months, however, are dry. These dry months can be hard on people as well as things that grow. Gardens and parks suffer because the city tries to conserve water. People suffer from the choking, eye-stinging dust storms.

The lake bed upon which Mexico City is built is one natural feature that is difficult to see. As mentioned in an earlier chapter, the Aztecs began filling in the lake with sludge to enlarge their island community. Over the years, the lake was completely drained to allow for the city's growth. The lake bed is an unusual site for a city because it causes many problems.

The main problem is that the soil is like a sponge: it swells up when it's

The pyramids of the Sun and the Moon had already stood for one thousand years before the arrival of the Aztecs.

wet. During Mexico's rainy season, the soil absorbs moisture and swells up. This gives building engineers a real headache. If a building isn't heavy enough, the swollen soil can cause it to bounce out of the ground, just like letting go of a rubber duck under the

water. If a building looks lopsided, it's showing the effects of the shifting soil.

Another natural feature of the city that can't be seen is the seismic gaps. Seismic gaps are spaces between the earth's plates deep underground. Mexico City felt their presence on September 19 and 20, 1985. That's when the plates shifted and bumped into each other, causing massive earthquakes. Over nine thousand people died in what became the city's worst disaster. The seismic waves (8.1 on the Richter scale) traveled at more than 1,500 miles (2,424 km) per hour and were one thousand times more powerful than the atomic bomb dropped on Hiroshima. Looking at the ancient National Palace and the fifty-two story Pemex building, it is a wonder that they are still standing.

One seemingly natural feature that can be seen is air pollution. This feature is, in fact, partly caused by people. Automobile fumes and the belching smoke from factories get trapped in the valley, resulting in the worst pollution of any city in the world. It threatens the health of the people and is destroying magnificent old trees in Chapultepec Park.

The Suburbs

Mexico City has many suburbs. Lomas de Chapultepec is a wealthy area with grand homes in the foothills. North of the city are the Satellite Cities, which are acres and acres of middle-class homes. Netzahualcóyotl is a fast-growing slum that lies outside the Federal District of Mexico City. Mexico City has grown beyond the district borders so the outlying suburbs have a separate government.

The Pyramids

Mexico City is a blend of old and new cultures, but even outside of the city the past has been preserved. About 30 miles (48 km) northeast is the ancient city of Teotihuacán, the largest city in the Western Hemisphere about 1,500 years ago. When the Aztecs first saw the giant pyramids there, they named them the pyramids of the Sun and the Moon. These were holy places to the Aztecs. They believed the sun and the moon were born there after two gods sacrificed themselves by leaping into a fire. They also believed that the sun was carried into the sky each day by Aztec warriors killed in battle and carried to its rest each night by Aztec women who died in childbirth. Finally, the Aztecs believed that only the blood of human sacrifice could keep the sun from falling out of the sky.

Street of the Dead runs between the pyramids. It was covered with sand and dirt by the Spaniards in their attempt to destroy the Aztec religion. The excavated street today looks much as it once did except for the presence of vendors hawking souvenirs.

Guanajuato

Guanajuato, northwest of Mexico City, was a major Spanish colonial city. For three centuries, it was the silver mining capital of the world. It produced nearly one-third of the world's silver. You can explore the silver mine La Valenciana, which was excavated in 1558.

Guanajuato is a web of narrow streets and alleys. The most famous alley is called Callejón del Beso. Legend says that the alley is so narrow that two lovers, kept apart by their parents, were able to kiss each other from their windows on opposite sides of the street.

Guanajuato is rich with the history of Mexican independence. The first major battle for independence took place here. Led by Father Hidalgo, thousand of Mexicans flooded the city in September 1810 just days after Hidalgo's cry for independence.

Taxco

Southwest of Mexico City is Taxco, perched high in the hills of the Sierra Madre. Its look is Spanish colonial, with white stucco houses and red tile roofs. Going to Taxco is like taking a trip into the past. One reason is that the town was cut off from outside influence until a paved road was built in 1930. Taxco has been declared a national monument, which means that no modern buildings can be built there. Taxco has been called the City of 200 Shops. Many of these stores sell beautiful handcrafted silverwork known the world over for its fine quality.

The tiled roofs and whitewashed walls of Taxco are typical architecture of the colonial era.

Above: Popocatépetl is a 17,887-foot (5,452 m) active volcano. The name means "smoking mountain" in the Aztec language. Below: A silver pitcher and jewelry stand ready for sale in a Taxco market.

Ixtaccihuatl-Popocatépetl National Park

About 50 miles (80 km) east of Mexico City, the beautiful Ixtaccihuatl-Popocatépetl National Park can be found. Mountain expeditions travel to the peaks of the snowy volcanoes, *Ixty* and *Popo,* every weekend.

Special Events and Celebrations

Special annual events and celebrations draw visitors to the areas around Mexico City. There's a sailing regatta on Lake Avandaro near Valle de Bravo in February. The Fiesta to San Isidro (the blessing of oxen) in Metepec is held in May. During an August celebration in Puebla, churches are carpeted with fresh flowers. A regional dance festival is held in Cholula every September.

WORLD

CITIES

City in the World

Mexico City has a peculiar and complex relationship with the rest of Mexico and with Mexico's neighbors. Managing these relationships is a delicate balancing act.

The Government and Its People

As Mexico's federal district, Mexico City is the seat of the country's government. Because of this, the city is not part of a specific Mexican state. It is an independent area, much like Washington, D.C. is in the United States. Mexico City, however, has much more power over Mexican states than Washington, D.C. has over its individual states.

Mexico's government is called a republic, which means that the people elect their representatives. Under this system, the government's power is divided into three branches as it is in the United States: executive, legislative, and judicial. These branches are headed by the president, the legislature, and the Supreme Court. Mexico also has state governments, but the federal government holds most of the power.

Mexico has only one official political party, the *Partido Revolucionario Institucional* (PRI or Institutional Revolutionary Party). Elections are held, but with a single party, there is never any doubt about who will win. State officials are appointed. Many poor people of southern Mexico and the

Banners bear photos of candidates during a recent national election campaign.

middle classes of the north resent the government's lack of interest in their opinions. They say that most of the government's attention and money go toward developing Mexico City.

The greatest hardships are found in the rural southern states. Although the Mexican government has set up schools and health clinics, they don't meet the needs of the rural poor. For one thing, children of poor families don't usually attend school because they begin working or begging on the streets at a very early age. Also, there are not enough clinics, so about half the people in rural Mexico never see a doctor.

Even though Mexico City can't provide jobs and housing for everyone who needs them, the city still represents hope to many of the rural poor, half of whom are unemployed. Many of these people migrate to the city in the hope of improving their lives. But many more, proud of their Indian heritage, do not want to leave their homes to be absorbed by Mexico City. They hold onto the hope that one day there will be more land reforms and that they will finally own the land on which they work. The middle-class northerners are greatly influenced by the United States. They would like to have a democratic government and would like to see the government do more to encourage industry and create jobs.

The area that is Mexico City today has been the center of Mexican government since the Aztec Empire. From that time on, people in other parts of Mexico have resented being controlled by this city. It is surprising to many people that Mexico has not had a revolution since 1910. Amazingly, the government survived even the disastrous economic crisis of 1982. During that time, many people lost their jobs or suffered pay cuts while the cost of everyday goods, such as food, skyrocketed.

Mexico and the United States

Some people, especially in the United States, believe that the severe problems and unrest in Mexico will make its people turn to communism as a way to get reform. The United States is afraid of having such a close Communist neighbor. It has watched other Latin American countries, such as Cuba, come under the influence of Communists. Americans are afraid that if Mexico were to become a Communist country, the Soviet Union could place missiles there, close to the United States. Some people predict that it is only a matter of time before Mexico also falls into Communist hands because of the "domino effect." The domino effect occurs when one event sets off an entire chain of events. (If you've ever lined up dominoes on end and pushed one to make the rest fall, you'll understand this.) Other people say that the slow spread of communism means it is becoming less attractive.

The United States wants to maintain friendly relations with its southern neighbor. It has given considerable money to Mexico. This is a difficult situation for the Mexican people, many of whom do not like being so dependent on the United States. They need the American dollars that come from aid, trade, and tourism, but they don't like American interference.

An example of this occurred in 1979. Mexico accused the United States of "stealing rain." It happened when Hurricane Ignacio, which was headed toward Mexico, suddenly veered out

Citizens gather for a campaign rally.

to sea. Mexico had hoped the hurricane would bring rain to its drought-stricken regions. Mexico claimed that United States planes flew into the hurricane and diverted it to protect Florida's resort business and to force Mexico to buy grain from the United States. United States officials denied the charge. They said the planes were merely studying the hurricane.

Another way that Mexico asserts its

independence from the United States is in its relations with other countries. It does not always follow what the United States does in other countries. Instead, Mexico establishes its own relationships. For example, Mexico was friendly with the Cuban Communist government of Fidel Castro even when the United States was not.

Nowhere is the relationship between Mexico and the United States more strained than on the subject of immigration. Each year thousands of Mexicans cross the border into the United States by wading through the shallow Rio Grande. They seek jobs and homes in the United States. They are willing to accept low-paying jobs that American workers don't want, such as farm labor, assembly-line work, and so on. Many employers wish to hire these Mexicans because they can pay them less than American workers and seldom provide them with benefits such

Many Mexicans live in poverty. Here, a mother and child take shelter in a hut made of cardboard and scrap materials.

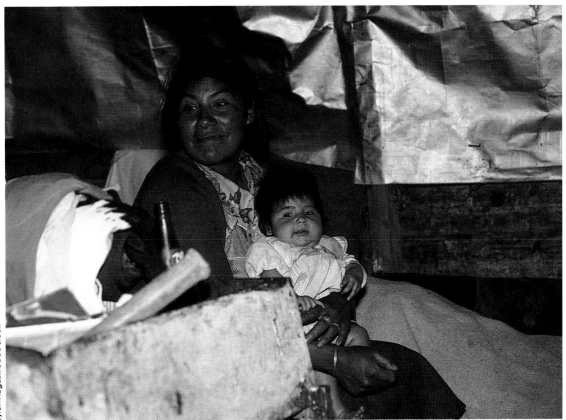

as health insurance or paid vacations. The employers know the Mexican workers won't complain because if government officials find out they're in the country illegally, they'll be sent back to Mexico.

Even immigrants who legally enter this country from Mexico face difficulties. American workers in low-pay-

Young people dance to the latest sounds at a disco called "The News."

DDB Stock

ing jobs are afraid that they'll lose their jobs. They know that immigrants will do the same job for less money. Some middle-class people resent paying taxes for the education and social services that large Mexican families need. Ideally, it seems that Americans would welcome the newcomers because they know that most Americans are descended from immigrants. But in reality, most immigrant groups—Chinese, Italian, Irish, African, and so on—faced discrimination similar to that which Mexicans face today.

Drug smuggling is another issue between the United States and Mexico. Large amounts of marijuana and some cocaine enter the United States from Mexico. Mexico has sent United States army troops into its border cities to help curb drug traffic. Meanwhile, the United States has tightened its border patrols. But Mexico does not totally agree with the way the United States is handling the problem. At times, United States customs officials decide to search every car that crosses the border, which causes traffic to back up for several hours. Mexico also thinks the United States should concentrate more on stopping drug use in the United States rather than trying to stop smugglers.

Even though Mexico and the United States have their problems, as neighbors they need to get along.

Some people say that Mexico is receiving only the worst aspects of American culture, such as fast food.

Mexico is the third largest trading partner of the United States. Europe, Japan, and Latin America are Mexico's other large export markets. Over the years, Mexico's balance of imports and exports has shifted. Until the 1940s, Mexico was heavily dependent on the United States for both food imports and manufactured goods. But with developments in agriculture and especially in manufacturing, Mexico became more self-sufficient.

Today, Mexico's major trading partners are the United States, Japan, Spain, the United Kingdom, and France. Of these, the United States does the most trading. In fact, Mexico exports twice as much to the United States as it imports. Crude oil and petroleum products amount to almost two-thirds of these exports. (As noted in an earlier chapter, oil and oil products are Mexico's greatest source of income.) Other exports include machinery, chemicals, fruits, and vegetables. Food products are Mexico's largest group of imports.

In terms of the degree of cultural exchange between the United States and Mexico, there is great imbalance. Unless you live in the southwestern part of the United States, you probably have not had much experience with Mexican culture. But in Mexico, even people in remote Indian villages know a great deal about the United

Many Mexicans fear the presence of foreign products, believing that these take markets away from Mexico's own companies.

States. That's because many of their television shows come from the United States and many schools teach English. In fact, the Mexican government is concerned that Mexico is becoming too Americanized. The northern Mexican states that border the United States are especially vulnerable to Americanization. American styles of dress, rock music, and slang are some of the signs that Mexican culture is heavily influenced by its northern neighbor. Another more disturbing sign to the Mexican government is the unrest among poorer Mexicans who see what they consider to be the wealth enjoyed by average Americans on television. The people wonder why they work so hard and yet have so little. The Mexican government cannot meet the demands of its people to improve their standard of living.

Mexico and Latin America

Mexico has considerable influence in Latin America. This country is the leader in the Contadora Group, which includes Venezuela, Panama, and Colombia. The Contadora Group, which first met in January 1983, works to bring peace to Central America. The Mexican government hopes to find peaceful solutions to political crises in Central America before the problems spill over into Mexico. Because of Mexico's experience in dealing with

For the young, American culture has a glamour absent in their own country.

Nighttime traffic circles the Angel of Independence monument on Paseo de la Reforma.

the United States, which is heavily involved in Central American issues, Mexico is greatly valued by other Latin American nations.

Mexico and the World

Historically, Mexico has not tried to influence the rest of the world. There is one exception to this—Spain. Mexico's relationship with this country has always been a hot issue. In the Spanish Civil War, Mexico fought on the side of the rebels and welcomed Spanish refugees. Today, there is still lively debate over whether the Spanish conquerors in Mexico were capable of "civilizing" the Indians they conquered. Some will argue that the Spanish Inquisition, in which thousands of non-Christians were burned at the stake, was just as savage as the Aztec practice of human sacrifice. The debate is the natural heritage of the mixed-blood Mexicans, who are descended from both the conquerors and the conquered.

Although Mexico has not deliberately tried to extend its influence to the rest of the world, it has nonetheless influenced it. Mexico's struggle to grow from a poor developing nation into a modern economically and socially healthy nation is being closely watched by the world. Will this spirited country, which has survived natural and economic disasters, be able to move forward against the population explosion that strains its resources? As one Mexico City official stated, "At the very least, we can be a lesson to the rest of the world."

Mexico City: Historical Events

1325 Aztecs establish the city of Tenochtitlán on islands in Lake Texcoco. Today, this area is the heart of Mexico City.

1502 Montezuma II becomes emperor of the Aztecs.

1519 Early this year, Spanish conquistadors, led by Hernán Cortés, land at modern-day Veracruz.

Cortés and his men enter Tenochtitlán in November. To gain control of the city, whose population is near 100,000 people, the Spaniards take Montezuma prisoner.

1520 Aztecs revolt against the Spanish control, killing hundreds of Spaniards in a battle that is now known as La Noche Triste. Cortés escapes.

1521 Cortés returns to Tenochtitlán, conquering the city and the Aztecs. Spanish rule begins in what Cortés calls "New Spain."

1535 The first Spanish governor arrives.

1553 The National Autonomous University is established.

1596 Effects of the Spanish Inquisition reach New Spain.

1810 Miguel Hidalgo strikes a blow for Mexico's independence with his speech, Grito de Dolores.

1813 José María Morelos organizes the first Mexican congress, which calls for independence.

1821 Spain grants Mexico its independence.

1822 Colonel Agustín de Iturbide is named emperor of the newly independent country.

1824 The country of Mexico becomes a republic.

Guadalupe Victoria is named its first president.

1833 General Antonio López de Santa Anna becomes president.

1847-1848 United States troops occupy Mexico City during the Mexican War.

1864 French troops, commanded by Napoleon III, invade and conquer Mexico.

1867 Napoleon III withdraws his troops, and Benito Juárez takes the presidency.

1877 Porfirio Díaz becomes president of Mexico.

1911-1917 Díaz's harsh leadership results in the Mexican Revolution, led by liberal leader Francisco Madero.

1912 Díaz is overthrown, and Madero becomes president of Mexico.

1913 Madero's general, Victoriano Huerta, overthrows Madero and has him killed.

1914 United States troops, backing Madero's supporters, seize Veracruz in a battle now known as the Veracruz Massacre.

1917 Venustiano Carranza, Madero's successor, directs the writing of a new constitution for Mexico.

1924 The Mexican government limits the power of the Catholic church.

1952 Benito Juárez International Airport opens.

1968 The Summer Olympic Games are held in Mexico City.

1975 An earthquake measuring 8.1 on the Richter scale hits Mexico City. Over nine thousand people die.

Mexico City

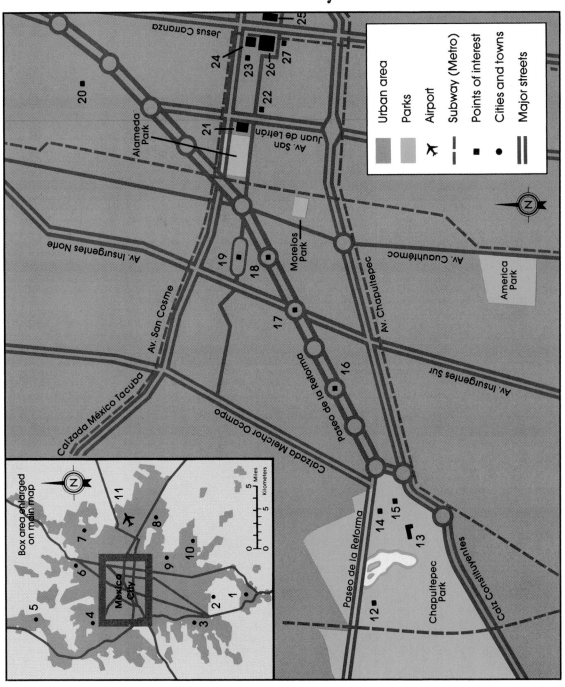

Legend:
- Urban area
- Parks
- Airport
- Subway (Metro)
- Points of interest
- Cities and towns
- Major streets

Jesús Carranza

Av. San Juan de Letrán

Alameda Park

Av. Insurgentes Norte

Morelos Park

Av. Cuauhtémoc

America Park

Av. San Cosme

Av. Chapultepec

Av. Insurgentes Sur

Calzada México Tacuba

Calzada Melchor Ocampo

Paseo de la Reforma

Chapultepec Park

Paseo de la Reforma

Calz Constituyentes

Box area enlarged on main map

Mexico City

Miles
Kilometers

Map Key

Mexico City Almanac

Location: Latitude—19.3° north. Longitude—99.1° west.

Climate: Mountain—cool and dry except in the rainy season. Average January temperature—54°F (12°C). Average July temperature—63°F (17° C). Average annual precipitation—29 inches (75 cm).

Land Area: 571 sq. miles (1,479 sq. km).

Population: City—9,682,500 people. Metropolitan area—approximately 15,000,000. World ranking—1. Population density—16,957 persons/sq. mile.

Major Airport: Benito Juárez International Airport—13,089,200 passengers a year.

Colleges/Universities: 38 colleges, universities and other institutions of higher learning, including National Autonomous University, Autonomous Metropolitan University, National Polytechnic Institute, Colegio de Mexico, and the Iberoamerican University.

Medical Facilities: Doctors—17,500. Nurses—27,200.

Media: Newspapers—main newspapers are *Novedades, Excélsior, La Prensa, Uno mas Uno,* and *El Universal.* Radio—30 stations. Television—6 stations.

Major Buildings: Latin American Tower—42 stories. Pemex Building—52 stories.

Transportation: 25 miles (40 km) of subway track.

Interesting Facts:

Mexico City has the oldest hospital in the Western Hemisphere.

Mexico City has the world's largest bullring.

The first printing press in the New World was established in Mexico City in 1539.

Index